CHICAGO
Portrait of a City

CHICAGO
Portrait of a City

GRAPHIC ARTS™ BOOKS

Library of Congress Control Number: 2005936449
International Standard Book Number: 978-1-55868-951-0

Captions and book compilation © MMVI by
Graphic Arts™ Books,
An imprint of Graphic Arts Books
P.O. Box 56118
Portland, OR 97238-6118
(503) 254-5591

Dust Jacket Design: Vicki Knapton
Interior Design: Jean Andrews

Printed in China
Third Printing

◄◄ Chicago's skyline rises behind colorful plantings in Grant Park.
◄ The Chicago River holds the reflection of a lavender sky at sunset.
► The lights of the city stretch to the horizon and a fiery sky.

◄ The *Flamingo*, a fifty-three-foot-tall
steel sculpture created by Alexander Calder, has
stood outside the Kluczynski Federal Building since 1974.
▲ A statue of children at play graces the area
in front of Navy Pier.

◄ The "forest" of the Magnificent Mile rises above a city with a population of nearly three million people. Atop the Hancock Center is an observatory offering incredible ninety-fourth-floor views a thousand feet above the busy city streets.
▲ Viewed from above, traffic near the Old Water Tower moves smoothly.

▲ The lakefront path allows one to enjoy
biking, inline skating, jogging, or just walking
along the lake. The one caution is to exercise good
judgment in sharing the the path with others.

▲ Clockwise from top left:

● A home decorates for Halloween with a jack-o'-lantern balloon.

● Giant Canada geese, *Branta canadensis maxima*, claim the Chicago area as their year-round home. Bountiful food sources plus a lack of predators have helped create a large population of these birds.

● Ivan Mestrovic's *Bowman* presides over the main entrance to Grant Park.

▲ One of 552 public parks in the Chicago area,
Grant Park incorporates walking paths through
nature's well-kept scenery, interspersed
with benches where one may rest.

▲ At the southwest corner of Millennium Park
(Michigan Avenue and Monroe Street) is Crown Fountain,
twin fifty-foot fountain towers. In addition to lighted cascading
water, the towers display video images of various Chicagoans.

▲ Michael Jordan is permanently
suspended in air in front of the United Center.
► A flag flies proudly before the 100-story John Hancock Center
building. Uses for the building include dining,
retail, offices, and parking.

◄ The Chicago River, a winding recreation area
utilized by numerous rivergoers, hosts various water
activities, ranging from kayaking (seen here) to sculling.
▲ Boats line up at Navy Pier on Lake Michigan.

▲ The Shedd Aquarium first opened to the
public in 1930. The aquarium houses some 650 marine
species, including such aquatic animals as Australian lungfish,
electric eels, octopus, penguins, sharks, turtles, dolphins, and whales.

▶ A beluga whale, *Delphinapterus leucas*, watches people watching it
at the Shedd Aquarium. Nicknamed the "sea canary" because of
its vocalizations, the beluga is an arctic and subarctic animal.

◄ Navy Pier is a playground for children of all ages—from two to ninety-two.

▲ CLOCKWISE FROM TOP LEFT: Chicago is a great place for fun and learning, including:

● Lakefront activities, like those on ocean beaches around the world;

● Climbing on a dolphin sculpture at the Brookfield Zoo; and

● Checking out a *Tyrannosaurus rex* named Sue—at
thirteen feet tall and forty-two feet long the largest
ever discovered—exhibited at the Field Museum.

▲ Whether you want fine or casual dining—eating in, take-out, or home delivery—Chicago offers it all.

▲ The ubiquitous coffee bar has
found Chicago, too. Here, prices of various
coffees are listed in the window.

23

▲ Founded in 1847, the *Chicago Tribune*'s first
print run was four hundred copies. The newspaper's
original building was a four-story structure built in 1869;
the present building, the Tribune Tower, completed
in 1925, reaches a height of 462 feet.

▲ The *Wendella* takes on passengers
for a sightseeing trip along the Chicago River.
One hundred fifty-six miles long, the river is spanned
by forty-five moveable bridges, built to allow
the movement of river traffic.

▲ The Spring Flower Show, one
of several seasonal exhibits, graces the
grounds at the Garfield Park Conservatory.
▶ High-rise buildings line the ever-
busy Chicago River.

▲ A Gothic church door offers
colorful respite from a hectic city.
► As most of the city gets ready for sleep, other
parts gear up for nighttime activities.

◄ The 6601 engine was delivered in
December 1979. The 6600 and 6601 were the first to
begin implementation of new standards of noise reduction.
▲ A man enjoys reading sitting next to a statue
"resting" on the same bench.

▲ The Chicago River lends
a charming ambience to a restaurant
situated on its banks.

▲ With buildings reflecting more
buildings that reflect still more, Chicago's
vistas take on an artistry that includes more than
just the architecture of its skyscrapers.

▲ Outside the Art Institute of Chicago, Lorado Taft's *Fountain of the Great Lakes* depicts five female figures arranged together so that water flowing from their shells parallels the passage of water through the Great Lakes system.

▶ The *Monument with Standing Beast*, by Jean Dubuffet, is a centerpiece in the plaza of the James R. Thompson Center. The twenty-nine-foot-tall, white fiberglass monument was given to the state by private donors.

◄ CLOCKWISE FROM TOP LEFT:
The city hosts numerous activities involving ethnic groups, including:
● A Native American Powwow (more than 10,000 American Indians live in Chicago);
● A Polish Festival, one of dozens nationwide, including street dancing; and
● A parade organized by the United German American Societies.
▲ The Chicago River changes its usual murky yellow-green
to Kelly green in honor of St. Patrick's Day.

▲ The Chinese Autumn Moon Festival pays tribute to the
moon goddess. Celebrated during a week when the moon shines
its brightest, the festival has been held each year in Chicago since 1997.
▶ A Chinese fair adds color and character to the city's streets.

◀ The flag of Puerto Rico is carried in a parade. A single white
star on a triangular field of blue, the flag also incorporates red and white
stripes similar to those of the flag of the United States of America.
▲ The Hispanic population is further enriched by
the Mexican-American community.

▲ The dome of the Cultural Center shows the exquisite
structure where so many concerts and other events take place.
▶ The Ford Center for the Performing Arts Oriental Theater
is a very glitzy place to go, black tie and all.

43

▲ Tulips, along with trees dressed
in new spring finery, line Michigan Avenue.
► The Chicago River is the happening
place for crew racing.

▲ A sailboat makes its way into Montrose
Harbor. Located five miles north of the entrance to
the Chicago River, the harbor offers more than six hundred
docks. Montrose Harbor is home to the
Chicago Corinthian Yacht Club.

▲ A pier, backdropped by Soldier Field, provides
safe harbor to numerous water-going vessels. The original stadium,
home of the Chicago Bears, was built in 1924 and named to honor American
soldiers who lost their lives in war. The new Soldier Field, which
has won several architectural awards, opened in 2003.

Regular $2.99 Jumbo $3.79

MILWAUKEE DOG
Bratwurst with brown mustard and sauerkraut

PITTSBURG DOG
chili and yellow mustard

ATLANTA DOG
Cole slaw, chili, mustard, ketchup, onion

LOUISIANA DOG
BBQ sauce, grilled onions, and tomato

CHARLESTON DOG
Cole slaw, chili, onion, mustard

GREEN BAY DOG
melted cheddar cheese

KANSAS CITY DOG
melted swiss cheese, sauerkraut and mustard

BALTIMORE DOG
deep fried dog with melted cheddar cheese and grilled onions

CORN DOGS	$2.19
POLISH DOG	$3.79
BRATWURST	$3.79
MINI CORN DOGS	$3.79

OTHER SANDWICHES

ITALIAN SAUSAGE $4.39
ITALIAN BEEF $5.39
ITALIAN COMBO $6.39
CHICKEN BREAST $4.95
SANDWICH $5.50

VEGGIE BURGER $3.95
CHEESEBURGER $4.69
SOUTHWEST CHICKEN $4.95

SIDES

▲ Hot dogs and baseball—
it just doesn't get any better than this.
All that's needed is apple pie to be everything American.
▶ Charles Weeghman built Weeghman Field in 1914 for the ChiFeds,
a team that played for the Federal League. In 1916, the Chicago Cubs, owned
by the chewing gum magnate, purchased the ballpark. It was renamed
Wrigley Field in 1926, and the Cubs have called it home ever since.

48

◄ Aptly named Oak Park is just one example
of a Chicago suburb with all the beauty of a park.
▲ A horse and carriage wait near the Old Water Tower, lit up
with holiday cheer. Carriage rides add a romantic touch.

▲ The Columbia Yacht Club, in existence since 1891,
is recognized as one of the leading sailing programs in the
country, giving sailors of all ages and skill levels the opportunity
to experience the thrill of mastering wind and water. Restaurant and
banquet facilities offer incredible views of the harbors and the city skyline.
▶ An aerial view shows the clock tower of the Wrigley Building. Constructed in 1920 by
William Wrigley Jr., the building serves as headquarters for the Wrigley Company.

◄ Scattered throughout the city, Chicago's
beautiful parks encompass approximately 7,300 acres.
▲ On this stretch of South Michigan Avenue, Chicago's elegant high-rise
buildings and verdant parks create a collage of color and design.
►► Fourth of July fireworks light up the skyline.

◄ A ticket agent for Trolley and
Double Decker Tours waits for customers.
▲ The O'Hare Airport Tower controls one of the nation's
major air traffic hubs, rivaling Hartsfield–Jackson Atlanta
International Airport as the world's busiest airport.

▲ The Adler Planetarium and
Astronomy Museum encompasses more than
35,000 square feet of exhibits, which range from scale
models of the solar system to astronomical
instruments to interactive adventures.

▲ Situated in a peaceful corner of
Grant Park, the Rose Garden offers a quiet
place to rest, reflect, and smell the roses
in Chicago's downtown green area.

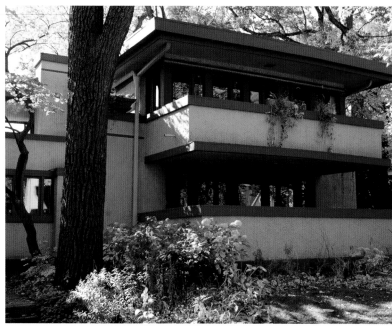

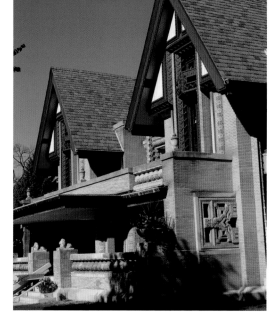

▲ Oak Park is famous for the world's
largest collection of Frank Lloyd Wright–designed
buildings and houses—twenty-five in all. The community
is marked by colorful homes, interesting architecture, and a
cozy, intimate family setting—a peaceful place to retreat
from the hustle and bustle of downtown Chicago.

▲ Frank Lloyd Wright (1867–1959), who
designed the Robie House in 1909, called the home
"the cornerstone of modern architecture."

▲ Seen from the Willis Tower,
the Hancock Center stands out against the skyline.
► The juxtaposition of textures, colors, and architectural styles
creates interesting patterns. The red structure is the CNA Building,
which houses the CNA Corporation, begun during World War II
to analyze data in an effort to help the Navy save lives
and use its scarce resources more effectively.

◄ Mounted police line up outside the Chicago Theatre.

▲ Opened in 1921, the Chicago Theatre was called "the wonder theatre of the world." Its exquisite lobby, staircase, and auditorium—embellished with murals above the stage and on the ceiling—still evoke the same awe expressed by early twentieth-century theatergoers.

▲ At 1,136 feet tall, the Aon Center is the only
rectangular building in the world that is more than
984 feet tall. Built between 1970 and 1972, it has changed
its name several times, starting as the Standard Oil Building and
later changing to the Amoco Building; it became the Aon
Center in 2003. This view is from Grant Park.

▲ The Osaka Garden is a traditional "stroll garden,"
a form first developed in the seventeenth century. Paths
lead visitors to varying vistas. The miniature island
is a key component of early Japanese gardens.

▲ One of the features at Lincoln Park is the Farm-in-the-Zoo,
which is a working reproduction of a Midwestern farm—from the
white picket fence to livestock to a tractor kids can pretend to drive. A glassed-in
animal nursery also lets people watch as volunteers help care for animal babies.
▶ Lake Shore Drive, adjacent to Lake Michigan, is guarded by tall buildings.
▶▶ Seen from the air, suburban Chicago stretches beyond the horizon.

▲ The Children's Museum at Navy Pier
is one of the city's top tourist attractions.
▶ In 1982, the Chicago Bureau of Architecture
erected the Children's Fountain in a traffic island at
the intersection of Wacker and Wabash. It has since been
moved to the northeast corner of Clark and North,
in front of the Chicago Historical Society.

◄ TOP TO BOTTOM:
◗ The doors of a CTA train open for passengers.
◗ A stairway and escalator at a subway station are uncharacteristically quiet.
▲ The first line of the Chicago "L" opened in 1892, starting a trend that
continues: most of the system is still elevated. However, some
subways have been added over the years; the first, in 1943.

77

▲ The Henry Moore sculpture *Sundial,*
erected outside the Adler Planetarium, is a style
of sundial called "bowstring equatorial." Shadows cast
on the "equatorial band" show the time.

▲ The Chicago Museum of Science
and Industry features some novel exhibits,
including a coal mine, "intelligent" LEGO bricks,
a submarine, and travel through virtual reality.

▲ Anish Kapoor's sculpture *Cloud Gate*
(known locally as the Bean) is made up of more than
100 reflective stainless steel panels, each in a unique shape.
Depending on the viewer's position, the sculpture's reflections
constantly change, creating fascinating shapes.

▲ The twenty-five-story Merchandise Mart
encompasses 4.2 million square feet and spans
two city blocks. The world's largest trade center was
opened by Marshall Field and Company in 1930.
Purchased by Joseph P. Kennedy in 1945, it was
managed by the Kennedy family until 1998.

▲ The *Windy*, a 148-foot, topsail schooner,
carries nearly five thousand square feet of sail.
The only certified four-masted traditional sailing vessel
in the United States, the *Windy* has an eight-foot
draft and a twenty-five-foot beam.

▲ Flags decorate the Michigan
Avenue Bridge as it crosses the Chicago River.
Built in 1920, the bridge and bridge house were designed
by architects Edward Bennett and Hugh Young. It was
designated a Chicago Landmark in 1991.

▲ A detail of the Chicago Stock Exchange shows
a beautiful building. When it opened for trading in 1882,
the initial offerings were eighty-two bonds and fifty-two stocks.
Today the Exchange has more than four thousand offerings.

▲ In 1973, Chicago became home
to the world's tallest building—the 1,450-foot
Willis Tower. Still the tallest building in North America,
it is the eighth-tallest freestanding stucture in the world.

▲ A unique statue designed by Lorado Taft depicts General George
Washington clasping hands with civilian financiers Robert Morris and Hyam
Salomon, men who gave thousands of dollars to support the American Army in the
Revolutionary War. The parking garage level of the Marina Towers forms the backdrop.
► A placid Chicago River flows past the Wrigley Building and the Tribune Tower.
►► The Beer Garden at Navy Pier offers a peaceful break from the
busyness of the fun activities available at the Pier.

◄ Old Town is one of the city's most unique
neighborhoods, known for its restaurants, shops, and
entertainment venues. Its historical streetlights and assorted
outdoor cafés invite visitors to experience all that Old Town has to offer.

▲ A metal sculpture by Frank Gehry forms part of the stage backdrop at the Pritzker
Pavilion in Millennium Park. The park is a 24.5-acre place to relax, play, learn,
and enjoy numerous attractions and activities in the heart of Chicago.

▲ A child pets an iguana at the Brookfield Zoo. Covering 216 acres, the zoo
includes tram tours, a butterfly garden, and a play zoo, among other features.

▶ TOP TO BOTTOM: Entertainment takes on unique possibilities:

● Young people on Chicago's West Side use fire hydrants
to help cool off during a deadly summer heat wave.

● A community memorial for Eleventh District police
killed in the line of duty includes a tug of war.

◄ The yearly Chrysanthemum Show is a
colorful highlight of the Garfield Park Conservatory.
▲ Masts from boats in Montrose Harbor outreach
the skyscrapers in the background.

▲ When Eli Bates died in 1881, he left
$10,000 for a park fountain, so Augustus Saint-Gaudens
and his assistant, Frederick William MacMonnies, were commissioned
to create a fountain in Lincoln Park. Completed in 1887, the resulting sculpture
strongly shows MacMonnies's influence. The fountain's flamboyance and
spontaneity are so vivid that park officials placed a fence around it to
prevent people from frolicking with the fountain's creatures.

▲ A glass roof creates its own interesting
artwork, reflecting whatever—and whoever—
is beneath it in its own unique way.

▲ CLOCKWISE FROM TOP LEFT: ◗ The Navy Pier
Flyover has done much to enhance safety and access on Chicago's
eighteen-mile Lakefront Path, one of the nation's busiest multiuse paths.
◗ Outside the Lincoln Park Conservatory stands a bust of preeminent maestro
Sir Georg Solti, conductor of the Chicago Symphony Orchestra from 1969 to 1991.
◗ The Jay Pritzker Pavilion, an outdoor concert amphitheater, seats 4,000 people
in fixed seats, plus an additional 7,000 on the Great Lawn.

▲ The Chicago Breakwater Light helps
show the way into the harbor. Placed in the harbor in 1918, it
was fully automated in 1979. Though larger vessels generally use radar
or GPS technology, smaller craft still key off the lighthouse to aid in navigation.
►► The Great Hall, Union Station's waiting room, has a vaulted ceiling that soars 112 feet.
Designed by Daniel Burnham, the building was completed in 1925, renovated in 1992
by Lucien Lagrange Associates, and declared a Chicago Landmark in 2002.

▲ The *San Marco II*, situated in the plaza
of One Financial Place, is a copy of a similar statue
by Ludovico de Luigi that once stood in front of St. Mark's
Basilica on the Piazza San Marco in Venice.

▲ A pair of stately lions flanks the Michigan
Avenue entrance of the Art Institute of Chicago. The lions
were sculpted by Edward Kemeys (1843–1907).

▲ Among other activities, Nobel Neighbors
support and coordinate the renovation of older homes
to make single-family homes available to low-income people.

▲ Buckingham Fountain turns brilliant colors at night.

◄ The Rookery Building, designed by Burnham
and Root, was completed in 1888; its lobby was redesigned by
Frank Lloyd Wright in 1905. It was designated a Chicago Landmark in 1972.
▲ Although Picasso never visited Chicago, his footprint is seen—in the sculpture dubbed
the *Chicago Picasso*. The artist himself granted it as a "gift to the people of Chicago."
►► The State Street Bridge, built in 1949, spans the Chicago River.

▲ The Azalea Show is just one of the brilliant flower shows at the
Garfield Park Conservatory. With both indoor and outdoor exhibits,
the conservatory encompasses some four and one-half acres of the park.
▶ A wall at Grant Park is embellished with massive concrete flower pots.
▶▶ Morning sun reflects off the 333 Wacker Building, one of the world's most
popular all-glass skyscrapers. Its curved wall of green glass follows a bend
of the Chicago River. The Willis Tower is prominent in the background.